WITHDRAWN

16.⁻

5/10

HYDROPOWER
Making a Splash!

Amy S. Hansen

PowerKiDS press
New York

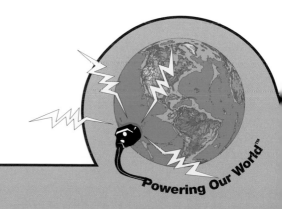

Powering Our World™

For Hugh, Nancy, Elisabeth, and Jeff

Published in 2010 by The Rosen Publishing Group, Inc.
29 East 21st Street, New York, NY 10010

First Edition

Editor: Amelie von Zumbusch
Book Design: Greg Tucker
Photo Researcher: Jessica Gerweck

Photo Credits: Cover, pp. 5, 7, 9, 11, 13, 17, 19, 21, 22 Shutterstock.com; p. 7 (inset) © Rob Shone/ Getty Images; p. 15 © Jan Stromme/Getty Images.

Library of Congress Cataloging-in-Publication Data

Hansen, Amy.
  Hydropower: making a splash! / Amy S. Hansen.
      p. cm. — (Powering our world)
  Includes index.
  ISBN 978-1-4358-9329-0 (library binding) — ISBN 978-1-4358-9746-5 (pbk.) — ISBN 978-1-4358-9747-2 (6-pack)
  1. Water-power—Juvenile literature. I. Title.
  TC146.H36 2010
  621.31'2134—dc22

                              2009024982

Manufactured in the United States of America

CPSIA Compliance Information: Batch #WW10PK: For Further Information contact Rosen Publishing, New York, New York at 1-800-237-9932

Contents

A river rushes under a bridge. Ocean waves swell. The outgoing tide pulls water back from the shore. All this moving water has energy. When we capture and use this energy, we call it hydropower. In the past, people used hydropower to turn waterwheels. Now we use it to turn **turbines** and make electricity. To make electricity, the water has to be moving fast. Sometimes we use water flowing over a waterfall. Other times, we build a dam so we can control the water's flow.

Hydropower is a clean, **renewable** energy source. We do not use up the water. We simply borrow its energy.

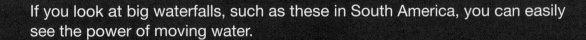

If you look at big waterfalls, such as these in South America, you can easily see the power of moving water.

Water is always moving. Every **molecule** of water on Earth is part of the water cycle. This is the pattern of changes that water goes through as it moves across Earth's surface and through the **atmosphere**.

You can see liquid water in rivers, oceans, and puddles. The Sun warms this water. This makes some water molecules evaporate, or turn into a gas called water vapor. As water vapor rises, it cools and **condenses** into clouds. When clouds get heavy, rain or snow falls. Rain and melted snow flow into streams and rivers. The cycle continues, powering turbines around the world.

6

You can see the rain pouring out of this cloud. *Inset:* This drawing shows how water moves through the water cycle.

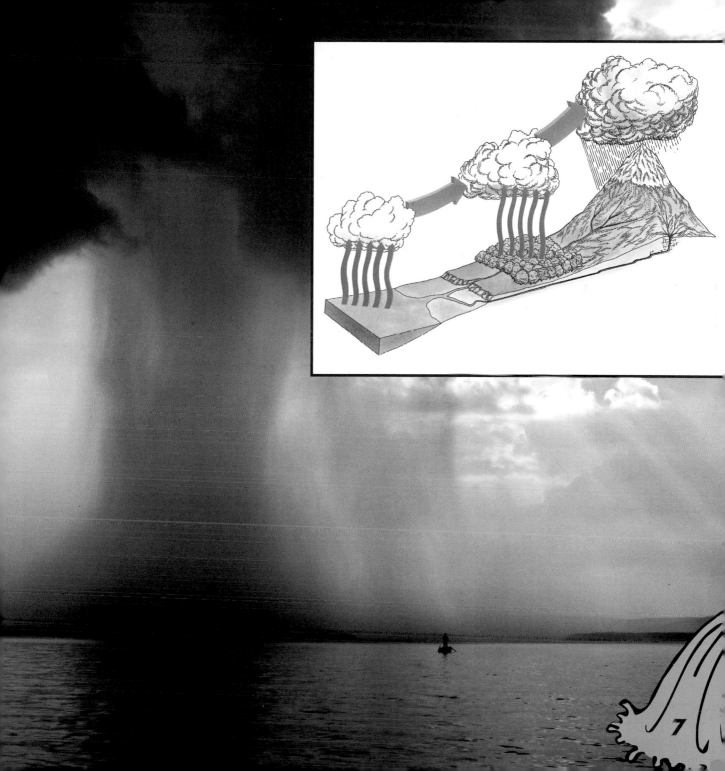

Waterpower Through History

The water cycle has been around for billions of years. Several thousand years ago, people started using waterwheels to capture moving water's energy. Ancient people used waterwheels to do many useful things, such as grinding grain for flour, cutting wood, and operating **bellows** for making iron. In about 65 BC, a Greek poet even wrote a poem honoring waterwheels! People in ancient India, China, and Syria used waterwheels, too.

Hydropower was important in American history. It powered mills to grind grain and weave cloth. In 1880, people made electricity using a water turbine for the first time in Grand Rapids, Michigan.

Mabry Mill, in Meadows of Dan, Virginia, was built in 1910. Today, it is still used as a grist mill, or a mill that grinds grain into flour.

Most **hydroelectric** plants are along big rivers. For example, the Niagara River, in Ontario, Canada, and New York, supplies lots of electricity. Every second, more than 530,000 gallons (2 million l) of water shoot over Niagara Falls, dropping 167 feet (51 m). Upstream and downstream, hydroelectric plants produce electricity.

When rivers do not have waterfalls, **engineers** may build dams. Dams hold back a river's water and form bodies of water called reservoirs or lakes. Dam operators let water out through pipes in the dam walls. The falling water spins turbines. These turbines turn **generators** that make electricity.

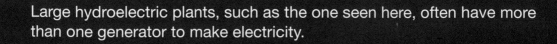

Large hydroelectric plants, such as the one seen here, often have more than one generator to make electricity.

11

The Mighty Hoover Dam

The Hoover Dam, on the Colorado River between Colorado and Nevada, has a huge hydroelectric plant. This big dam is 726 feet (221 m) tall. When the dam was first built, the Colorado River filled up the reservoir, called Lake Mead. Lake Mead is 110 miles (177 km) long.

To get electricity, engineers let water from Lake Mead flow into pipes. The water falls, spinning turbines that make electricity. The water then continues down the Colorado River. The Hoover Dam produces enough electricity to power a city of 750,000 people. The electricity goes to Arizona, California, and Nevada.

A total of 21,000 people worked on building the Hoover Dam. They finished building the dam in 1935.

Waves are another form of water energy. Waves form when wind pushes on water. Some engineers use waves to create electricity.

One way to use waves is to build channels that force waves together. This makes the waves more powerful. The waves can then turn turbines, which generate electricity. Another system uses buoys, or floats, with special pumps inside. The buoys change the bobbing energy of the waves into electricity. The electricity travels to the shore through wires running along the bottom of the ocean. The U.S. Navy set up buoys like this off the coast of Hawaii to supply power for a base.

14

People have been aware of the power of waves for many years. However, we are still learning how to use that power.

15

Scientists have also found ways to make electricity from the tides. Tides are changes in water level at the seashore that happen several times a day. They are created by the tug of the Moon's **gravity** on the oceans.

In France, people make electricity using a barrage, or small dam. When the tide comes in, water is caught in the dam. The water then goes out slowly, spinning turbines on its way. This system produces enough power for 200,000 homes. Engineers in the Philippines are planning a tidal fence. It would use a line of underwater turbines to produce electricity from the rising and falling tides.

Tides are stronger in some places than others. One of the places with the strongest tides is Canada's Bay of Fundy, shown here at low tide.

Problems with Hydropower

While hydroelectric power is clean and renewable, it can still hurt the **environment**. Building big dams floods large areas with water. These places were once home to plants, animals, and, sometimes, people. In some cases, the dams mean millions of people have to leave.

Dams also change the courses of rivers, making it hard for fish to move. Some hydroelectric plants build fish ladders, which help fish move past the dam. Dams can also cause mudslides and other problems. This happens because water is heavy. If the new lake is put in a spot that cannot hold up the water's weight, ground at the lake's edges can cave in.

When Glen Canyon Dam was built, the land upriver was flooded. People were angry because natural and historic places were covered in water.

19

Most of Earth is covered with water, so scientists will likely keep finding new ways to capture its energy. Some engineers are working with small dams. These dams cause fewer environmental problems than large dams. There are also tiny, or micro, hydroelectric systems that villages use to produce a little electricity.

Engineers want to capture the energy in small waves, too. One system uses a water-filled tube called the Anaconda. When the water ripples, a bulge forms, moves down the tube, and spins a turbine. The turbine powers a generator. Who knows what the next form of hydropower will be?

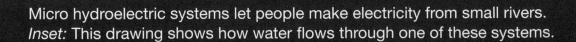

Micro hydroelectric systems let people make electricity from small rivers.
Inset: This drawing shows how water flows through one of these systems.

21

Hydropower Timeline

200	Waterwheels are used in China to make strong iron.
1877–1878	Lester Pelton invents a new kind of water turbine. It is used to run machines during the California **gold rush**.
1882	Appleton, Wisconsin, becomes the first city in the United States to use hydroelectricity.
1936	The Hoover Dam starts producing electricity.
1967	The new La Rance Tidal Barrage starts producing electricity on the Rance River in Brittany, France.
1978	The U.S. Supreme Court rules that dams cannot flood the homes of **endangered species**. Construction on the Tellico Dam, in Tennessee, is held up and a fish called the snail darter is moved.
1982	A tidal energy system opens at the Bay of Fundy, in Nova Scotia, Canada. It produces enough electricity for 6,000 homes.
2008	The Portuguese put a system known as the sea serpent into the ocean to collect wave energy for electricity. It is removed in March 2009 to fix problems.
2009	Scientists use wave power to move tools around the ocean so that they can listen to whales.

Glossary

atmosphere (AT-muh-sfeer) The gases around an object in space. On Earth this is air.

bellows (BEH-lohz) A bag with handles that lets out a flow of air when it is opened and closed.

condenses (kun-DENTS-sez) Cools and changes from a gas to a liquid.

endangered species (in-DAYN-jerd SPEE-sheez) Kinds of animals that will likely die out if people do not keep them safe.

engineers (en-juh-NEERZ) Masters at planning and building engines, machines, roads, and bridges.

environment (en-VY-ern-ment) All the living things and conditions of a place.

generators (JEH-neh-ray-turz) Machines that make electricity.

gold rush (GOHLD RUSH) A time in history when people found gold in the ground.

gravity (GRA-vih-tee) The force that causes objects to move toward each other.

hydroelectric (hy-droh-ih-LEK-trik) Making electricity from the energy of flowing water.

molecule (MAH-lih-kyool) The smallest bit of matter possible before it can be broken down into its basic parts.

renewable (ree-NOO-uh-bul) Able to be replaced once it is used up.

turbines (TER-bynz) Motors that turn by a flow of water or air.

Index

Web Sites

Due to the changing nature of Internet links, PowerKids Press has developed an online list of Web sites related to the subject of this book. This site is updated regularly. Please use this link to access the list:
www.powerkidslinks.com/pow/hydro/